Ladybird Learners
PLANTS

Contents

Plants are amazing – they can be all sizes, shapes, and colors and can live in many different places. This book explores the exciting world of plants, covering everything from beautiful orchids to the strange meat-eating sundews and Venus's-flytrap.

Acknowledgments:
The publishers would like to thank Wendy Body for acting as reading level consultant and The Royal Botanic Gardens, Kew, England, for advising on scientific content.

Photograph credits:
Page 38, Ardea; page 41, J. Allan Cash; pages 6, 21, 23, 40, Bruce Coleman Ltd; page 37, International Institute for Cotton; page 36, Malaysian Rubber Research Company; page 38, Science Photo Library.
Designed by Anne Matthews.

LADYBIRD BOOKS, INC.
Auburn, Maine 04210 U.S.A.
© LADYBIRD BOOKS LTD 1991
Loughborough, Leicestershire, England

Printed in England (3)

Plants

Written by ANITA GANERI

Illustrated by JANE PICKERING

Ladybird Books

Plants Around Us

There are over 375,000 different types of plants in the world. They range in size from the tallest trees to the smallest **algae**, which can be seen only with a microscope.

The largest living plant is a giant sequoia tree. It stands 362 feet tall.

Many algae live in ponds or ditches. *Chlamydomonas* is less than a five-hundredth of an inch long.

Plants can grow on land and in the water, in the freezing cold and in scorching heat.

Cacti grow in places where water is scarce. The largest cacti are the saguaros. Their thick stems and branches store water.

The Arctic poppy grows close to the ground, where it is protected from bitter wind and cold.

Prehistoric Plants

The first plants lived in the oceans 3 billion years ago. By 300 million years ago, plants were growing on land. Thick, steamy forests covered much of the earth.

The ginkgo is one of the early trees that still survives.

These early plants were very tall, with strong stems but no flowers.

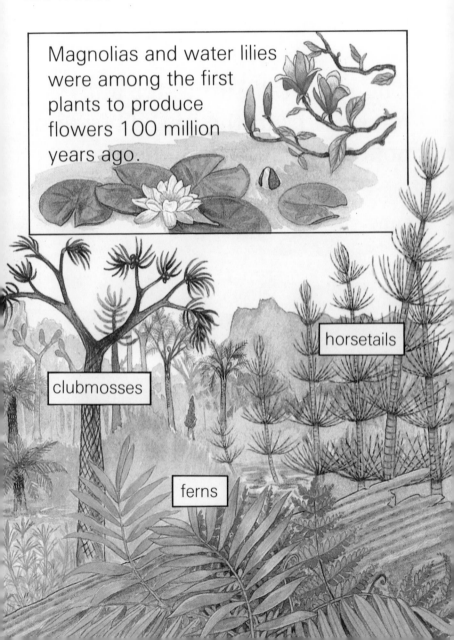

Magnolias and water lilies were among the first plants to produce flowers 100 million years ago.

clubmosses

horsetails

ferns

Roots, Stems, and Leaves

Many plants have roots, stems, and leaves.

The roots take up water and minerals from the soil. They also hold the plant firmly in place.

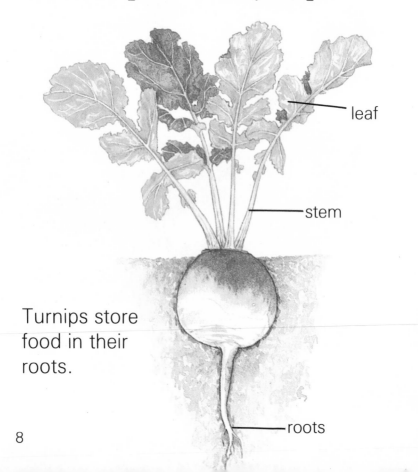

leaf

stem

Turnips store food in their roots.

roots

The stems hold the leaves up to the light.

Tubes in the stem carry water from the roots to the rest of the plant.

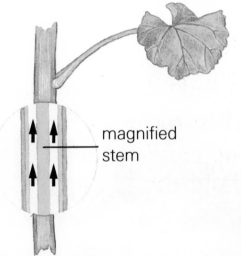

magnified stem

Most of the plant's food is made in the leaves.

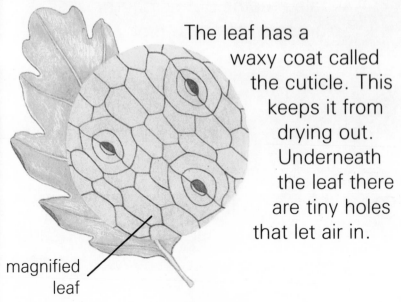

The leaf has a waxy coat called the cuticle. This keeps it from drying out. Underneath the leaf there are tiny holes that let air in.

magnified leaf

How Plants Make Food

Animals need to eat food, but green plants can make their own. Their leaves contain a special green substance called **chlorophyll**.

The way plants make food is called **photosynthesis**:

① The plant roots take up water and minerals from the soil.

② Animals breathe out carbon dioxide, which plants use to make food. The leaves take in carbon dioxide from the air.

③ The chlorophyll in the leaves uses sunlight to turn the water, minerals, and carbon dioxide into sugary food.

④ As they make food, plants release oxygen, which all other living things need.

④ oxygen out

② carbon dioxide in

③ sunlight

① water

① minerals

11

Flowers

Flowers make seeds, which can grow into new plants. **Pollen** must be taken from one flower to another for a seed to form.

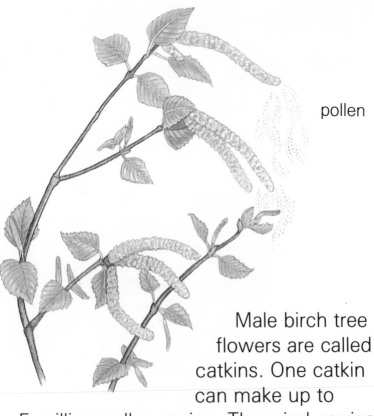

pollen

Male birch tree flowers are called catkins. One catkin can make up to 5 million pollen grains. The wind carries these grains onto female birch tree flowers.

Animals can move pollen from flower to flower.

1.
When a bee visits a primrose, pollen grains stick to its body.

seeds are formed here

pollen

2.
The grains brush off onto the next primrose flower the bee visits. The flower can then make its seeds.

13

Fantastic Flowers

Some animals are attracted to plants with large, brightly colored petals or strong scents.

Hummingbirds help pollinate hibiscus plants. The pollen sticks to their long beaks as they feed on the **nectar**.

The bee orchid looks like a female bee. It has furry flowers and wing-shaped petals. Male bees go to the orchid, thinking that it is a female bee.

Moths carry the pollen of yucca plants. The moth lays its eggs on the flowers. Later, its caterpillars feed on the new seeds.

The enormous flower of the rafflesia plant smells like rotting meat. This attracts flies expecting a tasty meal. Pollen sticks to their bodies when they land on the flower.

Seeds and Fruits

As a seed begins to grow, the flower dies.

Pits, nuts, and beans are seeds. The shells, berries, and pods they grow inside are fruits.

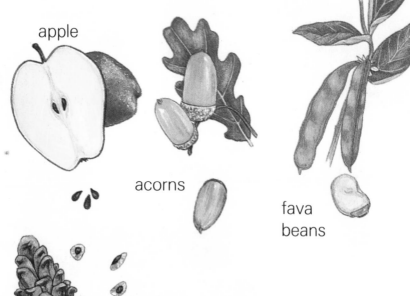

apple

acorns

fava beans

Pine cones are a type of fruit. As the seeds ripen inside, the cone scales harden and close. When they open again, the seeds are blown away.

Seeds can be many shapes and sizes.

In 1966 frozen Arctic lupine seeds were found in Canada. They were thought to be about 15,000 years old. Despite their age, they sprouted and grew into plants.

 Some of the smallest seeds come from orchids.

The coco de mer palm has the largest seeds. They can weigh as much as 45 pounds and can take up to 10 years to ripen.

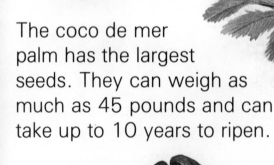

Traveling Seeds

Seeds contain tiny plants and a store of food. It is important for seeds to scatter so the young plants have enough space and water to grow.

Like pollen, seeds are scattered in different ways. Some are carried by the wind.

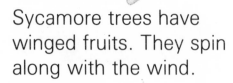

Sycamore trees have winged fruits. They spin along with the wind.

When the flower of a dandelion dies, its flower head becomes a mass of seeds, each with a tiny parachute.

18

Many fruits and seeds are spread by animals and birds.

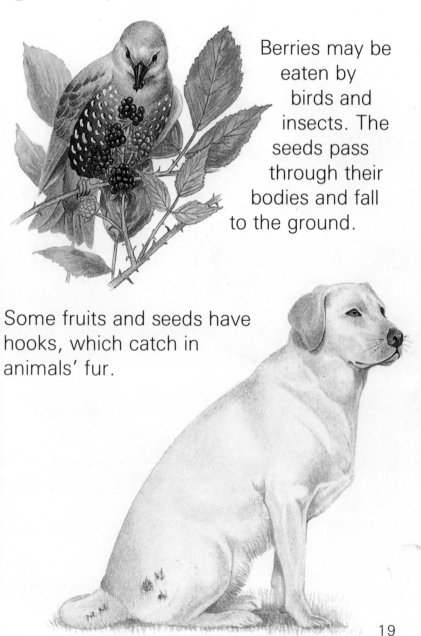

Berries may be eaten by birds and insects. The seeds pass through their bodies and fall to the ground.

Some fruits and seeds have hooks, which catch in animals' fur.

Trees

Trees are plants with thick, woody stems called trunks. They have bark to protect them from heat, cold, damp, disease, and pests.

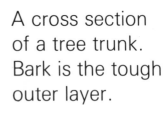

bark

A cross section of a tree trunk. Bark is the tough outer layer.

The number of rings across the section of a tree trunk tells you how old a tree is. In mild climates, a new ring grows every year.

One of the fastest-growing trees is the eucalyptus. It can grow an inch a day.

The Sitka spruce can take as long as 10 years to grow an inch.

This bristlecone pine tree in California is thought to be the oldest plant in the world. It is about 4,600 years old. The tree was alive when the ancient Egyptians were building the pyramids.

bristlecone pine

Types of Trees

There are two main types of trees — **conifers** and deciduous.

Fir and pine trees are conifers. They have sharp, thin leaves, called needles, on sloping branches. They produce their seeds in woody cones. Most conifers are evergreen. They keep their leaves during winter.

Oak and maple trees are deciduous. They have wide, flat leaves and a bushy shape. Nearly all deciduous trees lose their leaves in winter.

In autumn, the green chlorophyll in the leaves of most deciduous trees breaks down, and they turn red, brown, and yellow. Eventually the leaves die and fall off.

maple trees

Fungi, Algae, and Lichens

Mushrooms and toadstools are fungi. They do not have true roots or stems. Because they do not contain chlorophyll, they are not green and can't make their own food. They live off other plants and animals.

The dryad's saddle lives off tree trunks and stumps.

The fly agaric toadstool usually grows on the forest floor.

Algae include tiny pond plants and enormous seaweeds.

Pleurococcus is an alga. It grows on the moist side of tree trunks and looks like a green powder.

A lichen is two plants — a fungus and an alga. The fungus holds the plant in the ground. The green alga makes the food.

One type of lichen, reindeer moss, provides food for Lapland's reindeer.

Water Plants

Some plants can live in water. Some float on the water, while others live underwater.

The giant Amazon water lily has the largest leaves of any water plant. Thick ribs underneath the leaf help it float on the surface of the water. The leaves are strong enough for a person to sit on.

Seaweeds are algae that live in the sea. They provide food and shelter for many sea creatures.

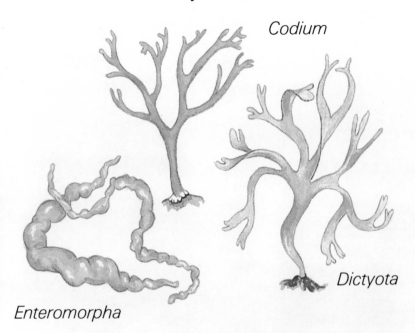

Codium

Dictyota

Enteromorpha

This knotted wrack lives on rocky seashores. It has gas-filled bubbles to help it float near the surface of the water.

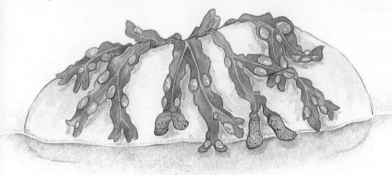

Desert Plants

Some plants can live in hot, dry **deserts** where water is scarce.

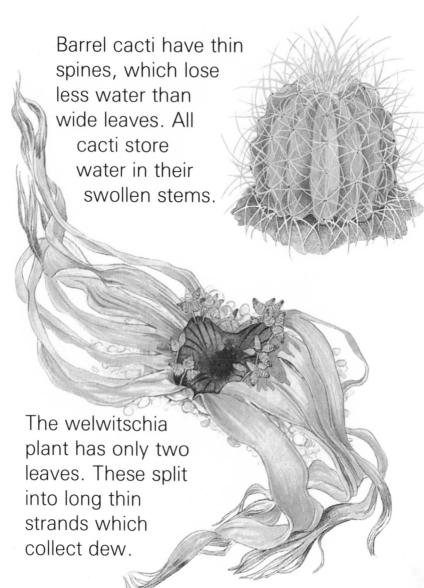

Barrel cacti have thin spines, which lose less water than wide leaves. All cacti store water in their swollen stems.

The welwitschia plant has only two leaves. These split into long thin strands which collect dew.

Other plants have huge underground roots.

The tamarisk tree grows in the Mediterranean, central Asia, and northern China. Its huge roots grow 150 feet into the ground to get water.

Mountain Plants

Mountain plants have to survive fierce winds and biting cold.

gentian

pink

Pinks and gentians grow very close to the ground in tight clumps. This protects them from cold, drying winds.

Because of the strong winds, some trees grow only 4 inches tall.

Mountain plants grow very slowly because they do not have a lot of energy. Many take over 10 years to flower.

A lichen on a rock may take 100 years to grow to the size of a postage stamp.

Alpine snowbell shoots give off heat to melt a patch of snow so the plant can flower even when the ground is icy.

Jungle Plants
Tropical rain forests contain thousands of different plants.

Orchids and ferns cling to high tree branches. Mosses and lichens cover the bark. Some climbers hang long roots down to the ground to get water.

Bromeliad leaves form a hollow which catches rainwater. Tree frogs and insects live in these pools.

Thick stems of liana plants hang down from the forest ceiling. Lianas attach themselves to young trees and are carried up to the sunlight as the tree grows.

The tallest trees can grow up to 225 feet high. Mosses and fungi live on the dark forest floor.

Plants That Feed on Animals

Some plants break down and absorb **(digest)** animals such as insects and frogs to improve their food supply.

Insects are attracted to the leaves of the Venus's-flytrap. When an insect lands, the leaves snap shut. They stay closed until the insect is digested.

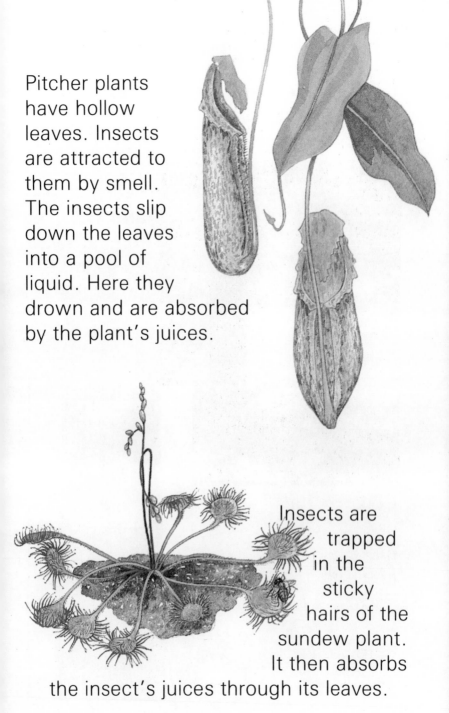

Pitcher plants
have hollow
leaves. Insects
are attracted to
them by smell.
The insects slip
down the leaves
into a pool of
liquid. Here they
drown and are absorbed
by the plant's juices.

Insects are
trapped
in the
sticky
hairs of the
sundew plant.
It then absorbs
the insect's juices through its leaves.

Useful Plants

Plants are used every day in many different ways.

Rubber is made from **latex** collected from cuts in the bark of rubber trees.

Cork oak bark is used to make bottle corks and mats.

Cotton is produced from the **boll** of the cotton plant.

String comes from fibers in the leaves of the sisal plant.

Black olive fruits produce a clear yellow oil used in soap making and cooking.

Plant Medicine

Plants have been used to treat illnesses for thousands of years.

The ancient Chinese found that ginseng roots were good for their health.

Many modern medicines were first discovered in plants.

Aspirin comes from the bark of the willow tree.

Quinine is used to cure **malaria**. It comes from the bark of the cinchona tree.

Plants are still used as medicines today.

Tea made from chamomile flowers helps people relax.

Eating garlic is supposed to lessen the chance of heart attacks.

castor-oil plant

Plant oils are also used. Castor oil is used in ointments. Eucalyptus oil helps soothe coughs and colds.

eucalyptus

Grasses

Grasses are one of the largest plant families. There are over 10,000 types. Rice and wheat are the grasses that are most important to people.

Rice and wheat are called staple foods because so many people eat them as a main part of their diet.

Rice needs plenty of water, so farmers grow it in flooded fields called **paddies**. This is a rice paddy in Asia.

About 350 million tons of wheat are grown each year. Most of this comes from the USA and USSR. Wheat is ground into flour to make bread.

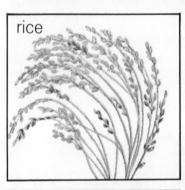
rice

corn

oats

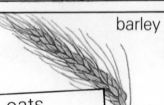
barley

Rice, wheat, corn, oats, and barley are called **cereal** crops.

Plants in Danger

Today about one-tenth of the world's plants are in danger of dying out.

Forests are being cut down for timber and to make room for buildings and farming.

Hedges are destroyed to make way for roads.

Pollution is killing many sea and river plants.

Fortunately, groups like the World Wildlife Fund are helping to save plants.

Some rare plants are grown in botanical gardens and then planted in their natural habitat.

Areas where important and valuable plants grow are being protected and made into **national parks**.

Glossary

algae Simple plants that contain chlorophyll but have no true stems, roots, or leaves.

boll The cotton seed pod, which bursts open when ripe.

cereal The seeds of a cultivated grass that can be used as food.

chlorophyll A green chemical that allows plants to make food in their leaves using light energy.

conifers Trees with needle-shaped leaves that produce their seeds in woody cones.

desert A region that has a limited amount of rainfall.

digest To convert food into a form that a plant or animal can use.

latex A milky liquid collected when the bark of a rubber tree is cut. It is used to make rubber.

malaria A disease spread by mosquitoes' bites. It causes fever and chills.

national park A protected area that is the home of important or rare plants and animals.

nectar A sugary liquid produced by some flowers to attract insects.

paddies Waterlogged fields where rice is grown.

photosynthesis The process by which green plants use the energy of the sun to make food.

pollen A fine powder produced by male flowers.

tropical rain forest A hot, rainy area with rich plant growth.

Index